HowExpert

How To

Your Step By Step Guide To Fencing

HowExpert with Christine Tanner

Copyright HowExpert™
www.HowExpert.com

For more tips related to this topic, visit HowExpert.com/fence.

Recommended Resources

- HowExpert.com – Quick 'How To' Guides on All Topics from A to Z by Everyday Experts.
- HowExpert.com/free – Free HowExpert Email Newsletter.
- HowExpert.com/books – HowExpert Books
- HowExpert.com/courses – HowExpert Courses
- HowExpert.com/clothing – HowExpert Clothing
- HowExpert.com/membership – HowExpert Membership Site
- HowExpert.com/affiliates – HowExpert Affiliate Program
- HowExpert.com/writers – Write About Your #1 Passion/Knowledge/Expertise & Become a HowExpert Author.
- HowExpert.com/resources – Additional HowExpert Recommended Resources
- YouTube.com/HowExpert – Subscribe to HowExpert YouTube.
- Instagram.com/HowExpert – Follow HowExpert on Instagram.
- Facebook.com/HowExpert – Follow HowExpert on Facebook.

COPYRIGHT, LEGAL NOTICE AND DISCLAIMER:

COPYRIGHT © BY HOWEXPERT™ (OWNED BY HOT METHODS). ALL RIGHTS RESERVED WORLDWIDE. NO PART OF THIS PUBLICATION MAY BE REPRODUCED IN ANY FORM OR BY ANY MEANS, INCLUDING SCANNING, PHOTOCOPYING, OR OTHERWISE WITHOUT PRIOR WRITTEN PERMISSION OF THE COPYRIGHT HOLDER.

DISCLAIMER AND TERMS OF USE: PLEASE NOTE THAT MUCH OF THIS PUBLICATION IS BASED ON PERSONAL EXPERIENCE AND ANECDOTAL EVIDENCE. ALTHOUGH THE AUTHOR AND PUBLISHER HAVE MADE EVERY REASONABLE ATTEMPT TO ACHIEVE COMPLETE ACCURACY OF THE CONTENT IN THIS GUIDE, THEY ASSUME NO RESPONSIBILITY FOR ERRORS OR OMISSIONS. ALSO, YOU SHOULD USE THIS INFORMATION AS YOU SEE FIT, AND AT YOUR OWN RISK. YOUR PARTICULAR SITUATION MAY NOT BE EXACTLY SUITED TO THE EXAMPLES ILLUSTRATED HERE; IN FACT, IT'S LIKELY THAT THEY WON'T BE THE SAME, AND YOU SHOULD ADJUST YOUR USE OF THE INFORMATION AND RECOMMENDATIONS ACCORDINGLY.

THE AUTHOR AND PUBLISHER DO NOT WARRANT THE PERFORMANCE, EFFECTIVENESS OR APPLICABILITY OF ANY SITES LISTED OR LINKED TO IN THIS BOOK. ALL LINKS ARE FOR INFORMATION PURPOSES ONLY AND ARE NOT WARRANTED FOR CONTENT, ACCURACY OR ANY OTHER IMPLIED OR EXPLICIT PURPOSE.

ANY TRADEMARKS, SERVICE MARKS, PRODUCT NAMES OR NAMED FEATURES ARE ASSUMED TO BE THE PROPERTY OF THEIR RESPECTIVE OWNERS, AND ARE USED ONLY FOR REFERENCE. THERE IS NO IMPLIED ENDORSEMENT IF WE USE ONE OF THESE TERMS.

NO PART OF THIS BOOK MAY BE REPRODUCED, STORED IN A RETRIEVAL SYSTEM, OR TRANSMITTED BY ANY OTHER MEANS: ELECTRONIC, MECHANICAL, PHOTOCOPYING, RECORDING, OR OTHERWISE, WITHOUT THE PRIOR WRITTEN PERMISSION OF THE AUTHOR.

ANY VIOLATION BY STEALING THIS BOOK OR DOWNLOADING OR SHARING IT ILLEGALLY WILL BE PROSECUTED BY LAWYERS TO THE FULLEST EXTENT. THIS PUBLICATION IS PROTECTED UNDER THE US COPYRIGHT ACT OF 1976 AND ALL OTHER APPLICABLE INTERNATIONAL, FEDERAL, STATE AND LOCAL LAWS AND ALL RIGHTS ARE RESERVED, INCLUDING RESALE RIGHTS: YOU ARE NOT ALLOWED TO GIVE OR SELL THIS GUIDE TO ANYONE ELSE.

THIS PUBLICATION IS DESIGNED TO PROVIDE ACCURATE AND AUTHORITATIVE INFORMATION WITH REGARD TO THE SUBJECT MATTER COVERED. IT IS SOLD WITH THE UNDERSTANDING THAT THE AUTHORS AND PUBLISHERS ARE NOT ENGAGED IN RENDERING LEGAL, FINANCIAL, OR OTHER PROFESSIONAL ADVICE. LAWS AND PRACTICES OFTEN VARY FROM STATE TO STATE AND IF LEGAL OR OTHER EXPERT ASSISTANCE IS REQUIRED, THE SERVICES OF A PROFESSIONAL SHOULD BE SOUGHT. THE AUTHORS AND PUBLISHER SPECIFICALLY DISCLAIM ANY LIABILITY THAT IS INCURRED FROM THE USE OR APPLICATION OF THE CONTENTS OF THIS BOOK.

COPYRIGHT BY HOWEXPERT™ (OWNED BY HOT METHODS)
ALL RIGHTS RESERVED WORLDWIDE.

Table of Contents

Recommended Resources 2

Introduction 5

Where Do I Get My Gear? 11

Types of Fencing 15

How to Build Your Own Battlefield 19

Type of Blades 21

Warming Up 33

Training Exercises 35

Practicing 72

How an attack sequence works 74

Care of your Equipment 86

Some places to look for equipment 98

Conclusion 100

About the Expert 103

Recommended Resources 104

Introduction

Have you ever wanted to sword fight? Fencing is a sport that can offer you not only the fun of swordplay, but also a decent workout.

Traditionally fencing was necessary training to protect oneself, one's king and country, one's honor, or the honor of a loved one. Swords in those days were very expensive to manufacture and a good blacksmith could take at least a year to make one by hand. The rich would receive the finest training and teaching that was available, while the poor often would not even have a sword, unless one was found on a battlefield or stolen. If you've ever watched a movie involving swordplay (well done swordplay) and thought that would be fun, you have the right idea. Fencing is no longer a sport that only the rich can afford. In fact, most anyone could get started with a modest budget, purchase a starter set and begin learning today.

With a modest investment of $200, you can begin your learning of the art of fencing as well. With proper maintenance and care your equipment will last for years, even with frequent use.

First, let's dispel the myths about fencing.

Myth #1: Fencing is a sport for wussies, pansies and wimps.

Nothing could be further from the truth. Fencing is an excellent cardiovascular workout. You can begin this sport at practically any level of fitness and the sport will naturally help the body increase endurance, flexibility and stamina. It is a great stress reliever and a challenging workout.

Myth #2: No one does it, or you must be part of an exclusive club to fence.

This is not true. There are community centers, some YMCA's, or better yet, if you have a group of friends that would like to do this together, you can train and learn together. There are books on fencing, and buying them will allow you to learn the sport together. Look for amateur tournaments in your area that you can compete in as you get better at the sport.

Myth #3: Fencing is dangerous.

Though you are swinging real metal swords at one another this sport is not that dangerous. It's actually one of the safest sports out there with the lowest amount of injuries as long as you follow the basic rules.

Rule 1: Proper equipment should be worn. This includes a proper mask, which must be worn. The mask could have a metal mesh faceplate, and should be the best Newton rating your wallet can afford. Any minimum protection mask will work, but remember you get what you pay for.

1. Your Fencing Mask

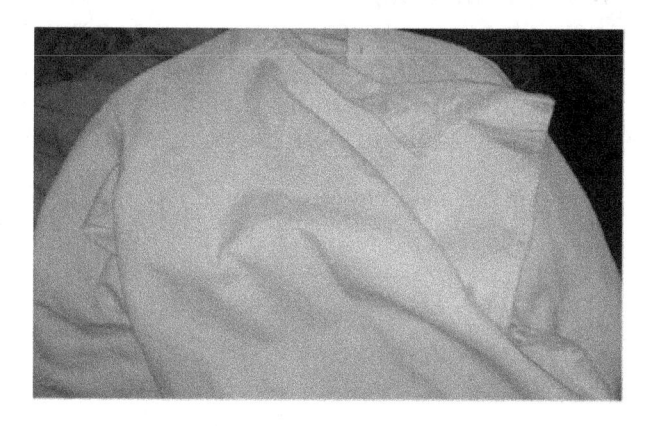

2. Fencing Jacket

Next, you'll need a proper jacket and glove for your sword hand. Quality and price will apply here as well.

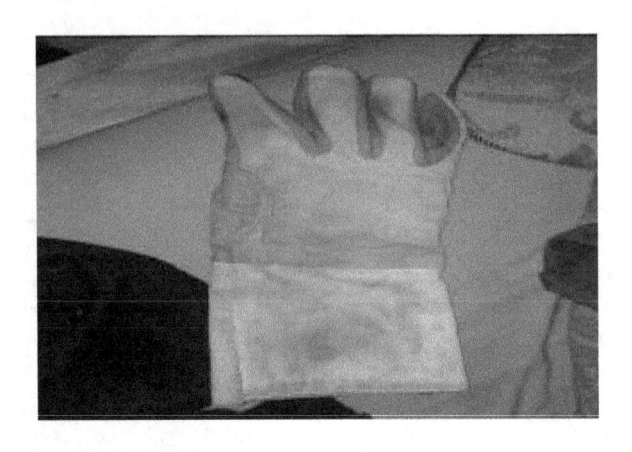

2. Illustration: A very well-worn Fencing Glove

Though it is not a required piece of equipment, I highly recommend using an athletic supporter. I've been fencing for over 20 years and if you're a male you should wear one. This is not something that comes up often, and is not required under the USFA (United States Fencing Association) or the written book rules.

3. Illustration: Fencing Outfit Worn by John Beeler

Remarkably, no book I've read on this subject has brought this equipment up either. Now keep in mind that it is not a valid target area no matter where you fence or what style you use. It would also be considered unsportsmanlike to tag your opponent in this region. However, after 20 years of fencing I will admit I've been tagged in that area a total of four times, and I can tell you from experience, wholeheartedly for less than a 20-dollar investment, it is worth every penny. However, again it is your choice.

For female students, a proper chest protector is required as well for the right reasons. This is in addition to the equipment that has already been mentioned.

Where Do I Get My Gear?

The answer to this question is simple. The majority of your equipment will be ordered online from companies that have equipment warehoused. You can look on the internet and once you get past the fencing construction links, you'll find sport fencing links. There are plenty to choose from; to narrow the list I could name a few companies I've purchased from in the past, but I am not endorsing anyone. Contact a local fencing club and see who they recommend you use as well. All equipment is serviceable as long as it meets the USFA guidelines. What this means to the customer is the following:

    1. It is safe to use in tournament.

    2. It is suitable for classroom or tournament fencing anywhere.

The best way to proceed once you've done your homework, and have found a company you like, is to purchase a starter set. This normally will range from around $150 to $200 dollars. A starter set typically consists of a minimum standard mask, jacket, glove and foil. Sizing is important since you can't walk into a store and try it on. Make sure that all measurements you've provided are correct.

Once you have your initial gear purchased and assuming you've grown to like the sport as much as I do, it is very inexpensive to continue. You'll mainly only need to order replacement blades and rubber replacement tips from here. Just as an approximation you're looking at a $40 to $50 investment for a good quality blade, and under $6 for a ten pack of tips.

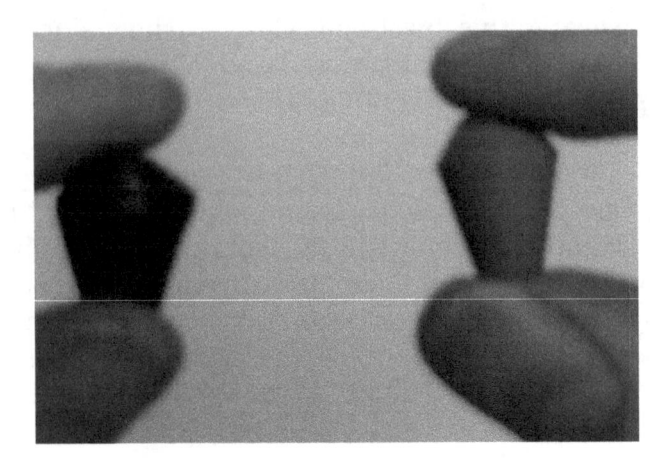

Figure 1: Tips for foil and epee

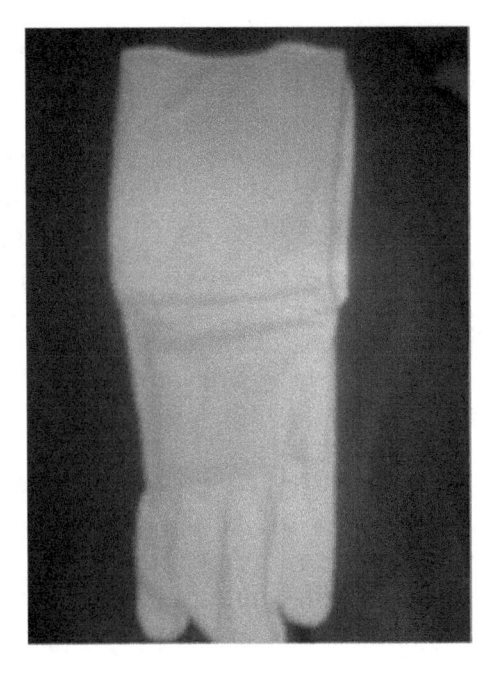

Real leather glove

Other items such as jacket, mask and glove should only be replaced as needed, (i.e. when your jacket begins to wear or starts coming apart. and you begin to feel every poke and prod severely) When your gloves no longer provide sufficient protection, they will need to be replaced as well.

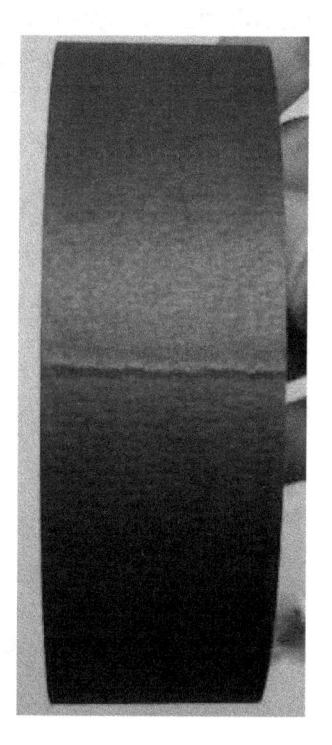

Figure 2: Blade tape

Blades that are on their last legs or are broken will also need to be replaced. You should never reuse a broken blade, or try and patch and reuse it; this is very unsafe. Masks should be replaced when dents occur and can't push it back out, or the mask has lost its shape. Pay attention to signs of rust you can't remove, this is another sign a replacement is needed. Those are spots where your opponent's blade could potentially penetrate your mask. Again, let me reiterate that it is a safe sport; however, you must properly maintain your equipment.

Basically, you wouldn't ride a motorcycle with a cracked helmet, and since your head will be with you your whole life, it is something that is worth protecting.

4. Illustration: Suited and Ready for Action

Types of Fencing

There are different venues for fencing as well as different types of blades; rules for each of them are distinctly different.

Venues for Fencing: Strip, Arena, and Free Range.

Let's begin with the battlefield; this is where your sword play will be done. It can be done indoors or outdoors (weather permitting). It would be preferable to play on a level playing field, free of debris, holes, divots, exposed tree roots or slippery surfaces (i.e. wet grass, leaves over grass, oil on pavement). A quick visual check just to be smart is recommended. This may sound ridiculous, but accidents can happen. I am a firm believer in an ounce of prevention.

The Strip: We'll begin with the fencing strip or piste (peeste). It's a length and width of 14 meters by 1.5 to 2 meters in width. That measures out to approximately 46 feet in length by 6 feet 7 inches in width. This is a bit wider than your average sidewalk and around six to twelve squares respectively.

However, for what I like to refer to as backyard or informal fencing, the length and width of the battlefield is up to the participants. If both parties agree, whatever you measure will suffice. But I would recommend the beginner and even the intermediate to stay as close to the parameters of a regulation strip as you can. If you desire at any point to compete in tournaments formal or informal or in a class room setting this will allow you to get used to the requirements because this is what is generally expected and required. Most instructors are normally going to stick to the standards that are in place. No one wants to be responsible for creating a sloppy fencer. This will also be the location where most beginners will build their core skills, including: developing footwork, distancing, timing and learning how to fight in a confined area. So, do yourself a favor and get warm and fuzzy with the strip before moving to the arena or open range styles of fencing.

Arena Style: In arena style or the round, you will use either a round or square ring.

A significant difference here is that strip fencing is linear, and both combatants move forward and backwards with a center point in the middle, side and back boundaries included, both players must stay in those confines.

5. Illustration: Proper Stance, with area that could be used for Arena fencing

In arena style, it is more three-dimensional and more resembles a duel-like scenario. You could circle your opponent, sizing them up, looking for weaknesses and trying to either score on them, or force them out of the ring. You can also use a combination of both methods depending on your battle strategy. Think of it as a three-dimensional chest game, it's constantly changing and you never know what your opponent will try to do next. These types of matches are a lot of fun; however, they most resemble a duel and are more enjoyable to watch as well. The rules of engagement can vary from location to location as well as instructor to instructor. Be sure to be well-versed in the rules beforehand. The size of the ring can vary, normally it will either be round or square. Stepping outside of the boundaries will cost you a point or even the match, depending on the house rules.

6. Illustration: Arena duel at Renaissance Fair

Free Range: The other venue is free range; this particular style is similar to arena style, with the exception being it requires much less set up time. Boundaries are larger and are much looser by interpretation too. For example, it could be any flat, park-like area outdoors. A concrete parking lot, a gym floor indoors or anything similar can work just fine. The parameters can be a general clearing, surrounded by a copse of trees, or any open area where you have a clear playing field to use.

Boundaries are usually determined by whatever existing landmarks are there to use. An example is a fire hydrant on one side and the sidewalk on the other side, or whatever you and your opponents decide to use.

How to Build Your Own Battlefield

If you decide you like strip fencing or arena style, creating your own playing field is very easy and inexpensive to do. Indoors a good solution is to have a role of blue painter's tape. Buy the widest available, this is a much cheaper alternative to fencing tape, and essentially the same thing. In a pinch, it can be used to replace a lost foil tip as well, and the fencing tape on your electric weapons too (this will be discussed later).

7. Illustration: John getting ready for tournament

Use of this tape is suggested because it doesn't lift surfaces, won't damage floors, and is very easy to put down and tear off, with no residue left on the floor, plus it costs pennies.

Outdoors you can use this on a sidewalk or parking lot

as a quick method. This tape does tend to lift if the surface is dirty. A better solution is sidewalk chalk, because it will come off with the first rain. You could also use a set of orange soccer cones, which are reusable, stackable, light and portable, and I've found to be a good solution also.

If you want to create an arena it can be done with cones, chalk, or even a partially buried rope. You could even conceivably use, in the right locations, outdoor paint that landscapers and construction workers use. However, be careful with where you use these items, what type of paint, and have consent or permission of someone authorized to give it. But generally speaking, a roll of painter's tape, a set of cones and a small box of children's sidewalk chalk should cover every possibility.

Type of Blades

Let's start with the basics, there are three types of blades, and I will proceed to describe each of them in

8. Illustration: Foil, notice the bend

detail. They are each employed differently and vary in size and weight.

Foil: This is the first type of blade, ranging in size from 0 to 5, depending on age and height. Size 5 is the longest. It's the most flexible of the three blades, and is also the blade that any reputable instructor will first teach you with. It is also the best weapon to begin your training with. The bell guard is small, about the size of a large coffee saucer, and the same shape. It does not offer much protection to your hand; therefore a proper glove is to be used.

The handle or grip can be one of several styles: French grip, Italian grip, pistol grip or sabre grip. Be aware that even though these grips will fit, to be tournament legal you'll need to use a pistol or French grip.

For informal fencing, you and your friends you can use what you like. For official use, we'll start with the French grip; it's the most classic grip. This is a straight grip with a slight bend to it. It is always placed up and to the right for the right-handed fencers or up and to the left for a left-handed fencer.

9. Illustration: Sabre grip

Pommels are sold in varying weights that can be chosen by the individual. The selections are available from any fencing vendors you'll find online, and you may need to experiment a bit to find the right one for you.

The shape of the foil is square, thick and unbending at the base, thin and bendy at the tip. The blade varies in strength incrementally from end to end.

10. Illustration: French

In foil fencing only the very tip is to be used. For scoring purposes, the target area is from below the neck to above the belt line anywhere on the trunk of the body, including the back. No arms, no legs, no head hits will count for points, thus they should not be aimed for, since they are not target areas.

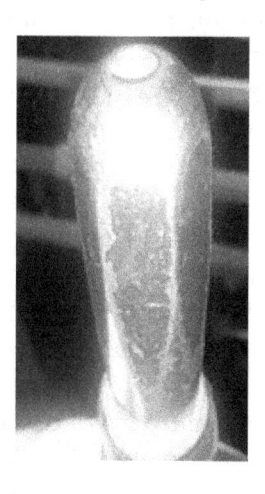

One type of pommel

For purposes of brevity, a point is a touch and a touch is a point. Most matches, regardless of the style will be played to five points. Every touch is worth one point. The first player to five points wins.

11. Illustration: Another type of pommel

In foil, the beginner learns to use the sword and how to use the different strengths of the blade to their advantage. The beginner will begin to learn blade control, first of their own blade, and later on with practice and proper seasoning of their opponents.

Bear in mind the foil should not be considered a temporary weapon, because the practitioner can always go back to basics and use it to strengthen any areas where they may have developed a weakness.

Epee: The next weapon we will discuss is the epee. It's employed much the same way as the foil. You only attack with the tip, using the sides of the blade to guard and defend.

The similarities are the length of the blade as well as the grip. However, the blade is heavier and stiffer, as well as the bell guard, which now offers more protection. How you employ the blade control is also different. It still exists but the blade does not flex as much.

12. Illustration: Foil Blade

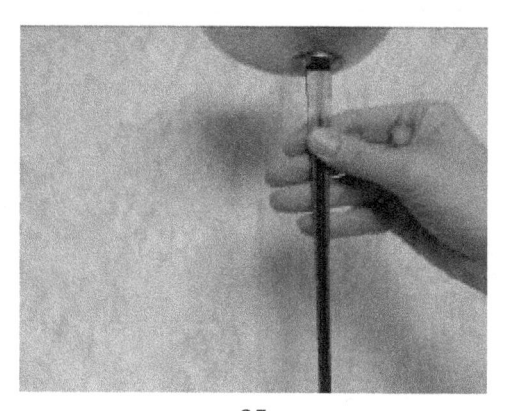

13. Illustration: Epee Blade

The guard is a soup bowl shape that is upside down and will provide you with better protection to the hand. That does not mean a glove should not be used, it is a must for fencing and being safe.

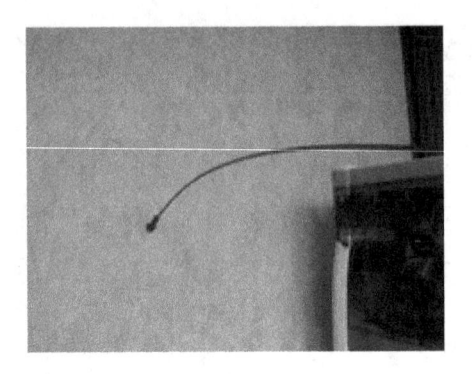

Epee Blade, less of a bend

At first use, your arm will get tired quicker and you will notice the point thrust will be stronger. Again, with proper equipment this is not a problem.

14. Illustration: Epee Bell guard

You may wish to wear a padded under-jacket, stomach belt and a thick t-shirt or a combination of the above when fencing with this type of blade.

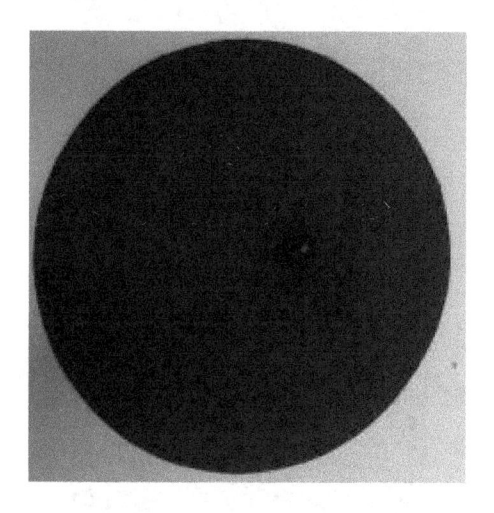

Figure 3: Epee bell guard pad

The shape of the blade is also different. It has been described as quadrangular in shape as opposed to square. The top or flat side has a groove running the entire length of the blade.

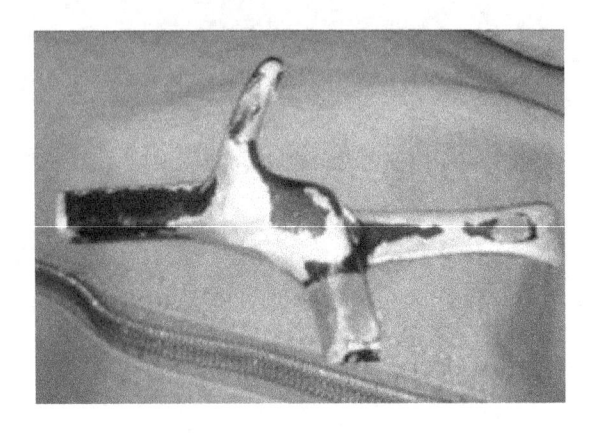

15. Illustration: Another style of pistol grip

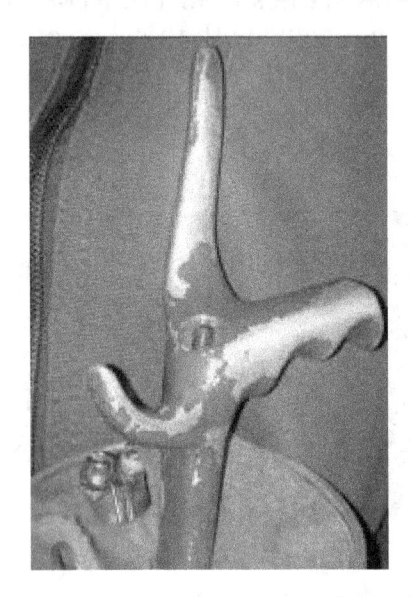

16. Illustration: Yet another style of pistol grip

Scoring is the same; however, your target area has now changed. Now you'll include your entire body, from the crown of your head to the soles of your feet. Front and back anywhere on the body, including arms and hands.

This changes the tempo of the game severely, since now arms and hands can be tagged. A touch to the knee or top of the foot, back of the head, anywhere you can earn or lose a point, if you don't properly defend or attack. In short, the whole body is fair game.

This style more accurately represents a duel, particularly in arena or free-range venues. Because the epee has a larger bell guard it can also be employed tactically as a small shield to deflect opponent's attacks where appropriate, giving you an extra advantage.

The first thing you will notice in fencing epee, after fencing foil, is the possibilities for tagging your opponent become limitless. Conversely the possibilities to tag you are equally limitless. Now it becomes a whole lot harder to defend; you have a whole body to protect now.

17. Illustration: Strike to chest valid in all forms of fencing

More fun, more challenging, and the next logical step in learning fencing.

Sabre: The third weapon is the sabre, which has elements of the other two blades, in the way that it is employed. However, it is important to note the differences as well. This blade has the whippiness of the foil, and some of the target area and tactical advantages of the epee.

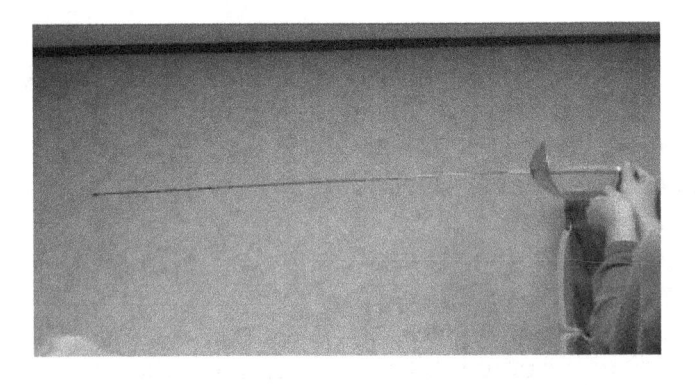

18. Illustration: Sabre Blade and Weapon

The similarities: A point is still valid to attack with; however, the blade is shorter. The sides of the blade can now be employed to use to collect points.

The guard is a cross between the epee and foil, and is typically referred to as a swashbuckler's or pirate's sword.

Grips on these are generally a sabre grip, which is

simply a short straight grip. Your blade is somewhat rectangular in shape, but thinner and curved at the end, and much whippier then the foil.

19. Illustration: Close-up Sabre Blade

An improperly trained sabreuerist game consists mostly of a lot of slapping with the sides of the blade. So be prepared for that, if you take up this weapon. A more balanced approach is to maintain the good tip control you learn with the foil and combine it with the edge of the blade employed in the sabre.

Scoring is the same as the other weapons. This weapon can be employed in the same venues as the other two blades. The target area is different though; now you score from only the waist up, from the belt line to the top of the head, as well as the back, legs, arms and hands are targets too.

I have been informed that the employment of this weapon had its roots in the Calvary days on horseback and that is why it's used in this manner.

Warming Up

To begin with flexibility is an important part of the game of fencing, and will help you avoid pulling a muscle. This is a sport you may begin at any level of fitness and flexibility.

20. Illustration: Strike to mask valid in epee and sabre

The more fit and flexible you are, the more enjoyment you'll get out of the sport as well. However, if you have any specific health concerns that you feel may limit or exclude your participation, talk to a doctor before taking up the sport. As with any exercise regimen, listen to your body and use common sense.

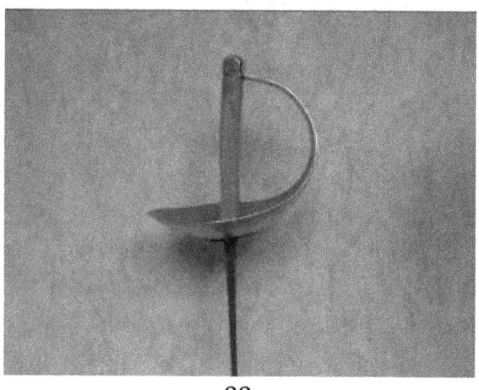

21. Illustration: Sabre Grip

Leg Stretches- Sitting on your bottom push your legs out as far as you can slowly and give them a good stretch. Do this a few times to warm up the muscles. From this position try to bend forward as far as you can. Remember to listen to your body if it's telling you to back off. Once you've done this to your satisfaction, stand up.

Find a wall or ledge to rest your hand on, put one hand on top of your foot and pull up. Stretching as far as you can will help you in the long run. Slowly pull up and hold gradually and let off as needed. Do this with both legs. Then reach for the sky and stretch as far as you can. Reach to the side and again stretch as far as you can.

Put your arms behind your back and move them upward as far as you can. In short you want to try to warm up as many muscle groups as you can, because this sport uses the entire body.

Also, be sure to keep hydrated and eat properly, and most importantly, have fun.

During this writing, I will be discussing a lot about rules and procedures, how to do this and when to do that. The goal here initially should be to have fun, not to turn the initiate into a rules lawyer. The rules are there to provide a framework and a standard scoring system. Keep these in mind as you move forward. Remember don't get frustrated, and we often learn as much from our mistakes as we do our success.

Training Exercises

Advancing and Retreating: Your feet should be positioned in the L-pattern. Depending on whether you are right or left handed will determine your lead foot. Assuming you're right-handed, your right foot should be pointed forward. Your left foot should be in back and pointed to the left, legs should be approximately shoulder width apart and knees slightly bent.

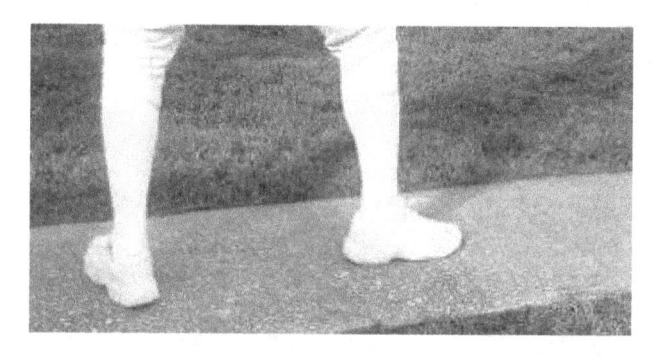

22. Illustration: Starting your Advance

To advance, extend your right foot out about six inches and slide your back foot forward so you are in original position, but forward a bit. In retreat, slide your back foot back six inches and bring your front foot back so your legs are shoulder width apart. (Distances may be less or more for movement, depending on your height).

23. Illustration: Moving forward for Advance

A good exercise to practice tip control is to suspend a tennis ball on a rope or string from a tree limb or a rafter in the garage.

24. Illustration: Final Advance position

Initiate should begin by trying to hit the center of the ball from a still position with a forward thrust. As skill level improves, it can be swing the ball back and forth like a pendulum and you try to tag it with forward thrusts.

Some other alternatives to this practice could be a practice bag, dummy or a tree in your front yard, instead of the above methods. You can put a piece of tape, mark, or draw with chalk and practice striking the same place repeatedly.

As your skill improves and you determine areas of weakness, move the spot to areas that you need to improve or where you are not hitting. When fencing, work on learning to cover areas where you tend to get hit a lot. Don't get frustrated, this is an ongoing learning experience.

25. Illustration: Practice with tree

When holding the grip, assuming it's a French grip, your thumb goes on top and the fore finger goes underneath as seen in illustrations. With a pistol grip, it's a bit different; it's held like a pistol, hence the term.

Be aware there are over a dozen different types of pistol grips out there. We do not have pictures of each grip, but only a few for you to see. The suitability of the grip is purely dependent on the preferences of the individual. I've tried them all and I prefer the French grip or the sabre grip, respectively. That is my choice and should not influence the choice of the reader. Experiment and have fun with this.

There are many grips, different weight of pommels, different bell guards. It may take you a while to find the pieces that work best for you. Virtually all of them are interchangeable, so it's up to you. However, if you find particular models and a combination that fits like a shoe for you, stick with it; you'll be happy you did. I recommend writing down the company you ordered from, and their part numbers. This will come in handy when ordering replacements. Very few parts except for the blades, have the model or part number on them so be aware.

B. Breathing control is another thing that you will have to work on. Remember that you need to breathe in through the nose and out through the mouth. If you don't breathe correctly you could risk hyperventilating. Remember it is best to take nice deep breaths when fencing.

26. Illustration: Pistol Grip

If you've had singing lessons or marital arts lessons, and you know how to breathe through your diaphragm, please do so. The idea is not to get winded, especially not faster than you have to. The bottom line is if you get out of breath too quickly in a match, you'll essentially become a human piñata. You may laugh at the mental image that this generates, but you will find out for yourself the first time this happens. Please remember these words, slow and steady wins the race. Concentrate, focus, conserve your energy, and use no movements until necessary. More precise you can move, the more thoughtful your movements, consistently, the better fencer you will become. I personally have defeated many opponents, and not necessarily, just because I was a better fencer. But because I got them to waste their energy on the strip, while I stayed calm, cool and collected. I kept my movement small, breathing under control, and focused on the prize. It disorients your opponent when they are flaying and jabbing at you from all sides and you're making small decisive motions, to block their attacks. For one thing, they wear themselves out quicker, and you will notice that they will leave themselves wide open.

27. Illustration: Salute at beginning of match sword up

This takes practice and training, and a lot of self-control. The most important thing to remember about the sport of fencing is you can begin this sport today, and you can literally spend the rest of your life shaping, and refining your techniques.

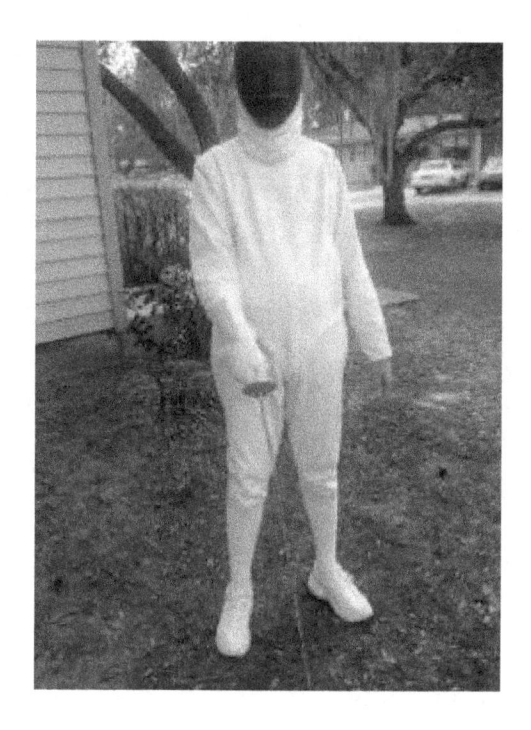

28. Illustration: Salute at beginning of match sword down

Unlike taking up the clarinet in fifth grade music class, your fencing gear could be something that will be with you for a lifetime.

XI. Attacks: Generally speaking, the perfect target area will be the center of your opponent's chest. There are various attacks that will be taught by an instructor to help you advance your strategies and techniques on the fencing field.

29. Illustration: Lunge

Lunges are one of the attacks that you'll learn. There are different types of lunges or different angles that you may lunge from in order to score a point on your opponent. Lunging is best done from a central position. You have the straight lunge; which is an attack towards the middle of the chest. Another lunge can be done from the side, either left or right. Lunges can be done from a low line or a lower position to an upward movement, around a forty-five degree angle.

30. Illustration: Lunge with strike

B. Advancing is the footwork, which is explained earlier in the book. Start with your front foot, depending on which is forward facing. You'll need to do the lunge or other moves at the same time as you are advancing.

C. Flechette or Fleche is a move you use in concert with your advance. It's essentially a running lunge attack. You charge your opponent on the strip, in an attempt to catch them off guard, as you run past them.

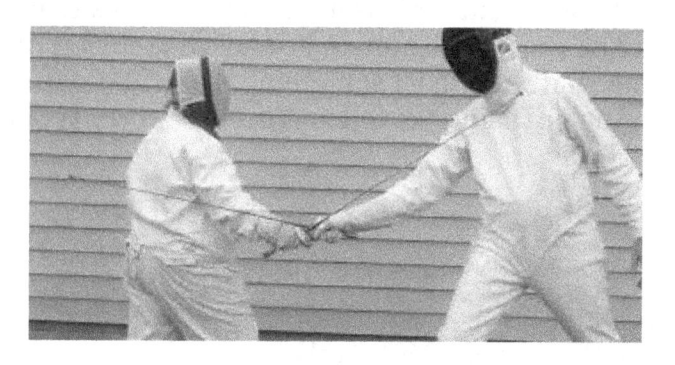

31. Illustration: Fletche in action

D. Flick is a technique where you deliberately bring your blade down and then up in a rapid motion. Essentially cracking the blade like a whip, in an attempt to get it to do an unnatural movement, and bend into an upside-down U shape to be able to tag your opponent on the back, shoulder, middle of shoulder blades or anywhere else you may be able to reach. This is a valid and legal move that can be used in all tournaments; however, I find it to be a dishonorable and deceptive technique. It is a move I refuse to use in my fencing. However, you need to be aware of it, because it is legal in all bouts, and many fencers do use it.

E. The running attack is something that is fairly easy to understand. Instead of a lunge you will run at your opponent and try to score your point. This is something that you may see in a match where a sabre is being used. It is not something that is wise to use in a match with a foil weapon. With this attack, you will have your arm extended out fully, meaning you could be left open for your opponent to score an easy point against you. Again, this is not really an attack that should be used by beginners just learning the art of fencing, and really isn't something that will be wise when you are using the foil and need to worry about right of way.

32. Illustration: Parry on low line

One thing about a counter attack is that the old saying is very true; sometimes the best answer is a strong offense. Learning the right ways to counter attack your opponents could often leave you in a spot where they are unable to score on you. Eventually, you may even wear them down and be able to pull off a great counter attack to win the match.

33. Illustration: Parry to outside

Counter attacks are another thing you'll learn if you want to do well in fencing. One counter attack is called the Riposte. Often this is referred to as "an echo of a parry." This is an attack you can use after you've successfully parried an attack. It is also the most common type of counter attack fencers will use. Since your opponent has just attacked you, you may be able to catch them off guard and undefended, thus using the riposte move to score a quick point.

34. Illustration: Parry to outside low line

You have a couple of different riposte that can be used either the straight or a direct; this is the one that most people will use. Basically, you'll use the same line that your attacker came in on and push your blade forward and attack them for your point.

35. Illustration: Parry to inside low line

Another type of riposte is indirect.. In this one, you will switch the lane and head in the opposite way from which your opponent came with their attack.

Another good move to learn is the stop thrust, or sometimes referred to as the "coup d'arret." You will use this either by performing a lunge or not; however, you should use this move on the first advance of your opponent. No matter if they attack you or not on their advance, this could be a good option that may have you with a point on your side. To do the stop thrust, fully extend the arm out that you hold your sword in. If your opponent is one who's moved forward with their arm bent, you could easily score that point with this maneuver. Try it with a lunge to get down a bit lower and perhaps under the parry of that opponent.

36. Illustration: Thrust

Also consider trying the time thrust, also known as the "coup de temps." This move will work best when using the lunge in conjunction with the maneuver.

37. Illustration: Another Thrust

If using the move or counter attack called the passata sotto, you'll need to move below the blade that is coming from your opponent.

This is considered a timing move, which is very spectacular to see in action.

38. Illustration: Foot placement, low block

Another counter attack you could use is called the tension. In this attack, your arm will be fully extended with the sword out. Not only will you block the blade, but you'll get the point at the same time.

The coup double, or a double touch is another counter attack that can happen during a match. If you and your opponent hit each other at the same time, it will be up to the judges to call the point. In many cases it will not be given to either of you, and the match will continue.

39. Illustration: Touch, valid in Foil

XII. Your defense with your blade is going to be based on your ability to block your opponent's blade and turn it into an attack.

40. Illustration: Invalid touch in foil

To do anything else would be absurd. If you need a better term, counter-punching fits. I personally have won many matches by deliberately waiting for the opponent to strike first.

41. Illustration: En Guard to Defensive position

You could learn an awful lot about your opponent by studying their moves, watching their body language, and inviting them to attack you. One excellent way to invite your opponent to do what you want them to do is deliberately leave a portion of your body open that you're particularly good at defending, in hopes that they will take the bait.

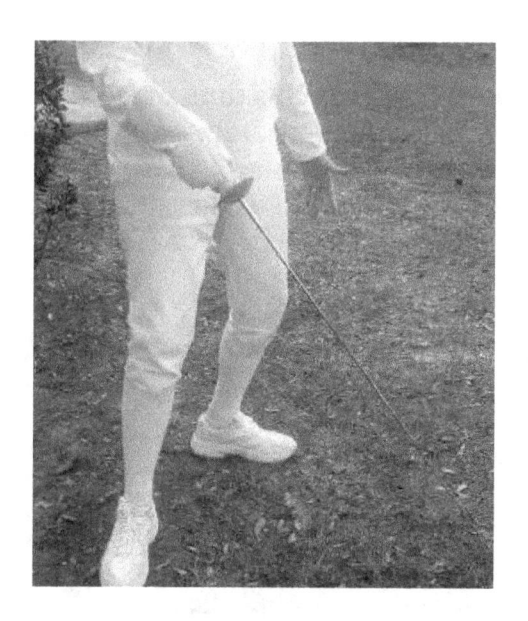

42. Illustration: Block to prime or lower position

For example, let's say you are excellent at covering, protecting, and blocking your lower right side. It would behoove you when setting the invitation to deliberately leave that part of your body unguarded, perhaps letting your blade dip or droop to the left.

43 Block upper position

Mind you, this facade may only work one time with an

opponent. Most of all remember that fencing is a thinking person's game, this thinking is one of the things that makes this sport fun. As you watch your opponent and study his or her moves, you're constantly putting battle strategies together in your head and changing them. This is based on their responses to your attacks and defenses.

44. Illustration: Block to seconde or lower middle

Like I said, fencing is a three-dimensional, three-hundred-and-sixty-degree video game, and you're in the center of it. Both fun, and a challenge. If you don't remember this and continue to progress, your game will be little more than two idiots slapping blades around.

45. Illustration: One example of a block

You should always consider your strategy to recover from an attack during a match. This could ensure that you don't get tagged for a point while trying to get your blade back in the right spot to defend, or your feet correctly placed. A proper recovery will not be you flailing around, looking like a fish out of water, but back, ready to defend and planning the next attack to make against your opponent.

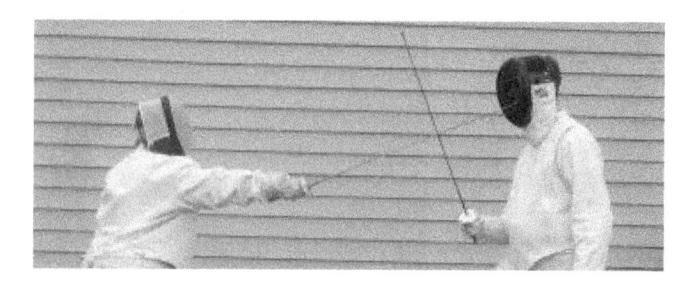

46. Illustration: Block of strike to mask

47. Illustration: Another lower block

A. If you remember, retreat movements were explained earlier in the book. These are very important, because at times, you'll need to give ground and back up, as well as times when you also need to stand your ground. Much of this will become instinctive as you become a better fencer. A lot of what is being discussed throughout this book will take a while to become instinctive. Don't be discouraged and don't deliberately challenge people that are way out of your league. That will only lead to frustration, unless you are okay with losing.

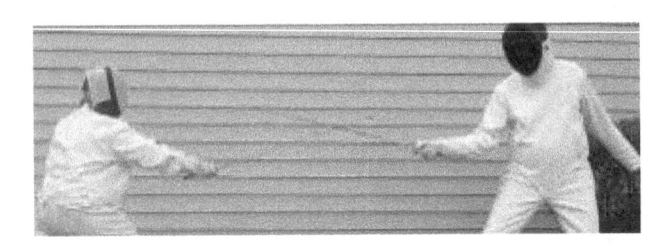

48. Illustration: Retreat with block

By the way, there is no shame in losing to a superior opponent, you could actually learn a lot by losing to someone who is better than you. While it's no fun to lose all the time, it is a good way for you to figure out where you rank among your peers. In the early stages, you will find it more enjoyable to compete against people in your skill area or close to it. Most instructors in a classroom setting will deliberately pair up people in this way so that you are not losing all of the time. Gradually they will pit you against better opponents as your skills increase. This one of the reasons why it's vitally important to become warm and fuzzy with your
footwork and weight of a
weapon in your hand. Don't switch around between a bunch of blades; find what feels good for you and stick

with it. Your sword should ultimately feel like an extension of your hand. Once you have a practice weapon that feels good for you, and you decide to get an electric counterpart, do your best to make it the equivalent of your practice weapon. A trick some Olympians use is to deliberately make their practice weapon slightly heavier than their electric weapon, so that when they get on the strip, they increase their movement speed.

49. Illustration: Parry example

B. A parry is essentially a block when your opponent's blade is coming at you. Always block from the inside to the outside. Otherwise you'll have to push the blade across your body to get it away from the target area. Keep your movements small. Fencing in real life is very different from the movies and TV shows that have a lot of sword play.

50. Illustration: Lower parry

Disregard all the wide, sweeping movements and flourishes seen in a lot of your Robin Hood, Zorro or other sword play movies. They look great on camera, but they will get you tagged and exhausted on the fencing court. In true dueling, these huge moves are almost never used.

51. Illustration: Upper parry

The reason being is you had two people trying to kill each other, with sharp pointed blades, do the math.

No one is going to leave themselves wide open, to get stabbed, and that's the way you need to think of it.

52. Illustration: Parry

When you are taught fencing, you'll most likely be learning the classical style. With this style, assuming you're right-handed, you have your right foot forward, left root pointed to the left, in the L-shape pattern. Legs shoulder-width apart, knees slightly bent, rocking back and forth on the balls of your feet.

53. Illustration: Classic fencing poses

Your sword hand will be out in front of you in the on guard (en garde) position. The left hand should be up, behind your head and parallel with your right ear, it will look much like a scorpion's tail. When you attack and lunge, the hand will drop down as a counter-balance, flat. This is the classic style of fencing.

The alternative is to have your left arm down by your side. When you lunge you will put your arm straight out to help you balance.

54. Illustration: Alternative fencing poses

The advantages and disadvantages of both:

Scorpion Style: Traditionally this is how fencing has been taught, most likely since the inception of the sport. Any instructors you run into are going to be familiar with the classic style, and will most likely teach you this way. Many people you compete with will use it as well. The downside of this style is to your opponent, any time you go to make a lunge, there is a split second where your arm drops, and you make the attack. This warns your opponent and is a great way to telegraph to them, what your next move is.

Alternative Method: There is an alternative to this, which is completely legal even though other instructors will argue this is not an appropriate method. Let yourself be the judge.

In the alternative method, your left hand is down by your side, and extended outward as a counter-balance as you lunge. The difference is from your opponent's point of view; they will not be able to see your back hand until after you've made the attack. As opposed to how your opponent could see your arm drop when you used the other method as you attacked. You will quickly learn in this game, that split-second movements are a lot longer and tell a lot more, when you're on the battlefield.

XIII. Strategies are essential to the sport of fencing if you plan on ever winning a tournament or even a match Block counter. One simple strategy you could use is included here: Wait for your opponent to attack. Then, counter their attack with one of your own. With each strategy, there are pluses and minuses. If you're fencing foil, you automatically give up right of way. Using epee there is no right of way to contend with. In either case the advantage of this strategy is to wait for your opponent to commit and then respond to their action, hopefully catching them off guard and scoring a point. Remember to vary your strategies; don't always be offensive or defensive. Your strategies need to be ultimately flexible and fluid in your mind.

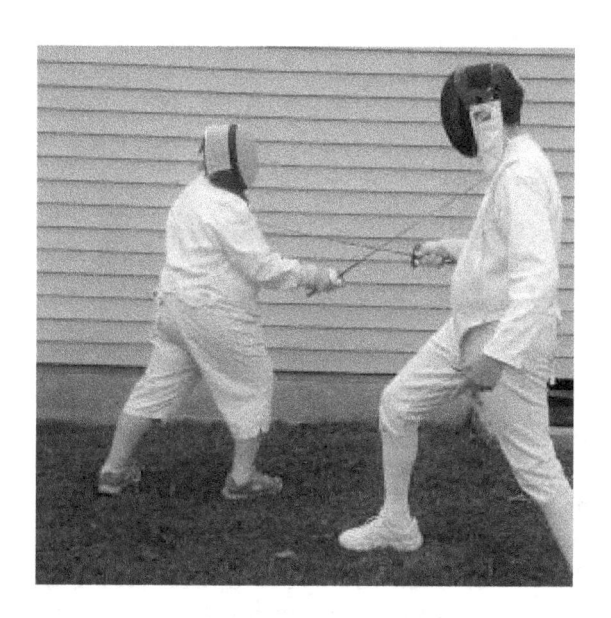

55. Illustration: Cross over with touch

Over under/ under over is another strategy you could use in a tournament. When on an attack, a popular strategy is an over-under, or the reverse, under-over attack.

What you'll want to do is get past your opponent's blade to their target area. You do this by either going over, under, or around that blade. Although this may seem rather obvious, it's more difficult then it appears with a skilled opponent. Some tips you can try: you can faint, do an over attack; when your opponent deflects, quickly pull your blade back quickly, ducking under and trying to score.

56. Illustration: Example of Over Under

Bridging is another alternative for attacks, and it's a useful one to use. In this method, blades clash, slide along the top or bottom of your opponent's blade, and you'll need to quickly duck under and tag your opponent.

Distancing can be another strategy to use. Keep both of your legs shoulder-width apart, when on the strip. Generally, try to keep yourself right out of the range where your opponent could tag you with his arm fully extended out. At some point, you will get a very good feel for this.

But knowing how to distance against your opponent is going to be crucial if you don't want to be tagged. Avoid sloppy technique: flaying about a blade is one very poor way to lose a point. Mad slashing is another thing to avoid, for several reasons. First and foremost being that no one will want to fence with you, making it hard to get your skills up. Second, you'll tire yourself out before you are even close to your target.

57. Illustration: Blades crossed, Christy parrying

When attacking and defending, keep your movements as small as possible. Don't telegraph; you want to have the element of surprise. Fencers fight differently, some are very aggressive and attack as soon as the match begins. Others are simply counter-punchers; they wait for their opponent and then respond. Others are a combination of the two. The best advice I can give you is to be unpredictable to your opponents.

58. Illustration: Disarming opponent beginning

Rules of Engagement: The rules are not the same for any of the three weapons, so they will be explained individually.

59. Illustration: Opponent disarmed

We will explain the similarities and the differences for each of the weapons.

60. Illustration: Blades engaged

Foil will be the first weapon we will talk about for rules of engagement. In foil, the first item you'll want to work on is your footwork. The L-pattern previously described involves advancing and retreating, lunging, parrying (deflecting your opponent's blade) and attacking, which primarily has to do with thrusting. Remember this is modeled after the rapier, which was a point-thrust weapon. Traditionally it was razor sharp at the tip, and the goal was to land your point at a target area that would be fatal: the throat, heart, lungs, stomach or any soft tissue, leaving your opponent dying or dead on the field.

61. Illustration: Not a valid touch in foil, too low

In foil, aside from lunging, thrusting and parrying, there is also a concept known as right of way. Right of way was designed for score keepers to be able to better determine who was entitled to the point.

Imagine, two fencers are on the field and both appear to strike and hit the opponent at approximately the same time. Who gets the point? Usually this can be broken down into determining who had right of way during the melee., It is no easy feat.

62. Illustration: Salute to opponent

Most practice matches have anywhere from one to three judges observing the match, and it can be quite challenging to determine who has earned the point in very close matches.

Right of way does helps decipher that in some situations. Here's a basic example: Two fencers are at the centerline on the strip. The coach or instructor says fencers on line, fencers ready, fencers fence, and combat begins. Whoever moves first in an aggressive posture or initially attacks has the right of way. He does not lose right of way until his weapon is properly blocked and deflected by the opponent. For example, the opponent on the left attacks as soon as the coach gives their command, and the right is defending. The opponent on the left has right of way while the opponent on the right-side steps and stabs the opponent on the left in the midsection; then, a split second later, the opponent on the left stabs the opponent on the right in the midsection. The opponent on the left has the point because he had right of way. It may not always seem fair, but this is how right of way works in foil in tournament.

And these rules are always observed. The disadvantage of right of way is that it does not emulate certain aspects of a sword fight. One argument is the opponent on the right would have skewered the opponent on the left, then he would have fallen, he would have died; and he would have lost the match. Now this may have happened in real life and that may have been how it would have ended. The theory behind right of way in foil fencing is to help train the initiate in becoming a thoughtful, careful and precise fencer. The logic behind right of way is based on the concept that if these were sharp blades and your life hangs in the balance in the choices and selections that you make, you're not going to make theatrical Hollywood type moves, and take unnecessary risks. And believe it or not, all the things you should learn when you learn foil make you a much better fencer when you begin fencing in epee and sabre. So, remember in right of way, somebody has to be attacking and somebody has to be defending. If you are defending you have to at least aggressively strike your opponent's blade before you stab them, that's all. The logic behind this is similar to the logic one would have participating in a real sword fight; you want to get your opponent's razor sharp pointy thing away from your body before you go in for the kill. The theory allows a double impalement to be avoided. In the real world during the times that these were done, the only person happy about the double impalement would have been the undertaker; he gets twice the business. In essence, that's how right of way works and why it exists. Keep in mind the sport of fencing is something you can spend a lifetime shaping and honing adapting and developing, point control, foot work, blocks, parries, attacks and defenses. At first a lot of your movements are going to be herky-jerky and clumsy. Have patience, and eventually you will train your memory muscles to respond how you want. It will happen faster than you think. Your feet will know where they need to be, and the sword will fall into your hand exactly where it needs to be, and it will feel like an extension of your arm. Right now, in the 21st century, this is an awesome time to get into this sport. The technology used in the manufacture of the weapons is excellent; the highly competitive nature of the sport is great for physical conditioning, mental keenness and stress relief. Think about it another way, you come home from work, wherever you work, whatever you do, and you like video games. Walk up to your game system, turn on your TV, grab your controller, plop in your game and begin playing. You can play against the computer or another opponent, but you're looking at a flat screen and using your brain a little bit, thinking some of the graphics on this game is incredible. And there is no doubt that it can be very fun. Now, instead of using a hand controller to manipulate a flat character on a flat screen, you're holding a sword in your hand and fencing against a breathing, thinking human being. As you adapt, learn, progress and get creative; so does your opponent. This aspect of fencing alone beats the living hell out of any video game with a limitation of moves and a limitation of options. No batteries are required, least not yet with practice gear. The equipment is durable, decent equipment you will be able to beat the living daylights out of. If you take care of it, keep it clean, free of rust and maintained, you can get years of enjoyment from even some of the more modestly priced equipment.

Rules of Engagement for the epee:

Epee should be the second weapon you learn. Everything you learned foil, including point control, foot work, parries, blocks and blade control, all comes into play here with certain happy advantages for the fencer. For starters, no longer is your target area limited to the torso. The whole body is now opened as a valid target, from the crown of the head to the soles of the feet. You can now score points when you tag. You no longer have a whippy blade at the end that is stiff at the blade. This blade is now stiff from tip to hilt, it doesn't bend. With blade control, both your blade and your opponent's blade, you become more skillful, instantly. Remember, you started with a whippy flexible blade that was hard to control, to a blade that is now much easier to control. To give you a better analogy, it's not unlike learning to drive a stick shift and then switching to an automatic. There is no longer a right way to worry about. The operating theory in epee is that whoever gets there first with the most wins is the winner. So, for the scenario described earlier in the previous chapter where opponent on the right struck first, his point would now count, and he would win the point. This is because right of way does not exist in epee at all. I will tell you many fencers that start in foil and develop those skills, switch to epee and never look back. Because they absolutely despise right of way, and the automobile antenna type whippiness of the foil blade. I personally still love all three; each style has its own challenges and I embrace them all. But please enjoy your own adventure and have fun with it. The scoring system in epee is the same scoring system as in foil; the first person to five points wins.

63. Illustration: Foot tag, valid in Epee fencing

Sabre rules of engagement: In sabre you do have right away once again, just like in foil fencing. However, the target area is now only from the waist up, and you may strike with the sides of the blade, as well as the tip anywhere on the trunk of the body, arms or head. Same footwork, same strip, but now your blade has teeth, on the sides of the blade as well. A good sabreuerist uses both the tip and the sides; he is not just a slap-happy idiot.

Now that I've given you a glimpse of some of the basics of all three styles, you can understand them a bit more. Let's go to the beginning of a standard, traditional fencing match. The variants will follow. Both fencers step out onto the strip or piste, and they will have their helmet tucked under their off arm, and they will be facing each other. Depending on the venue they will both don their helmet and salute the spectators, the judges and their opponent. Or they might salute the spectators, judges and their opponent, and then don their mask.

Practicing

64. Illustration: Block

One of the best ways to get improve your fencing is through practice. Though you may find that the normal classroom techniques don't always work, they will teach you the basics you need to know. There is a way to focus on more attacking and defending, on purpose. Get together with a friend who is around the same level of fencer as you, though anyone will normally work.

Now instead of just working on the normal, fake tournament type of thing, work on attacking only. That means you try and score a point, while your opponent only works to defend against your attacks. Not only will this help both of you out, but will give you a way to only work on one aspect of your fencing.

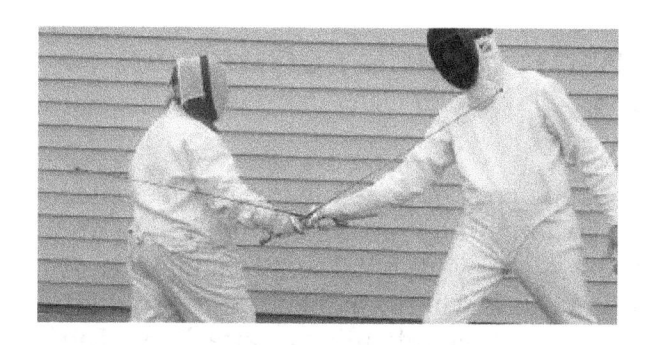

65. Illustration: Corpse de Corpse (cora-cora) lower

After you've done enough attacking, switch, allow your opponent to only attack while you defend. Doing this will knock out the counter attack moves and anything else that you may normally be working on, and will instead let you work on one thing at a time.

66. Illustration: Corpse de corpse (cora-cora) higher

How an attack sequence works

When facing your opponent your attack sequence should go something like this: You'll either attack, or you'll wait for your opponent to attack. In foil, assuming this is where you begin your training, you are now either defending or attacking. During a bout, you'll be continuously switching between the two parts. You will have no choice but to switch gears quickly from attack mode to defense mode. At some point, as your skills improve, it will be completely fluid and automatic. You won't even make the mental connection that you are attacking or defending; your memory muscle will have your body doing what it is supposed to. To use an analogy, it's like driving a car, where your brain assembles all the data mechanically. First you check the mirrors and adjust them, put your key in, etc., then at some point your body just knows what to do. Fencing is pretty much the same way.

67. Illustration: Going around for an attack

When either attacking or defending keep your movements small, avoid parries where you knock the blade way out of the park.

68. Illustration: Scoring on the back

Your opponent merely needs to not connect with you when he attacks. When attacking, vary the way you attack; deliberately try not to use a discernible pattern. Ideally, study your opponent's movements and look for an opening. Continuously scan for an area they don't protect as well as they should, and exploit it. If they do a very good job of protecting most of their body most of the time, you will have to be more creative and this is what adds challenge as well as more fun to the game. You can drop your guard deliberately in areas where you should protect to goad your opponent to attack you, it is a technique that works out well in some cases. This is also known as setting traps. Keep in mind; never underestimate how intelligent your opponent is. Also, be aware that every defense can be turned into an attack, just as easily as an attack can be turned into a defense.

As your skills improve, learn how to control your blade as well as your opponent's blade. This is one of the reasons why it is vital to begin with foil. Because the foil is extremely light and whippy at the end, but gets sturdier as you get close to the hand, it allows you to learn how to get a real feel with what you can do with your blade, along the length of it, as well as your opponent's blade.

For example, if you try parrying with the very end of your foil with the end of their foil, nothing will get accomplished, except you're likely to get tagged. Their foil is likely to bend and they can duck right under it and tag you. If you'd like to do an effective parry against your opponent, you need to strike with the mid-section of your blade, about half way up the blade, and strike their blade about half way up theirs as well. The closer you get to the bell guard on your opponent, the stiffer their blade gets, as well as that is the sturdiest part of your blade. Keep this in mind when attempting to do an effective parry.

Keep in mind you should also get in close. Fencing, as with any martial art, you cannot attack without leaving some part of your body exposed. The best you can do is what I call risk management. Meaning, try to leave as small of a part of your body open as possible, while doing your best not to telegraph your attack, and quickly strike before they do. Just make sure that you initiate right of way so your tag counts. Right of way can always be initiated, by making an aggressive move towards your opponent and striking their blade firmly. They are required to defend before they can attack.

This is one of the few advantages of the right of way rules, because later, if you were to start competing in epee there is no right of way. The weapon is employed very similarly; however, there is no right of way, and there is no weak portion of the blade. The blade does not bend or give very much from end to end at all. This will then add in new challenges to the game. The preferred order of learning how to fence is to first begin with the foil, follow with the epee, and end with the sabre.

Foil teaches you all the small movements and fine motor control as well as helps you hone your footwork along with attacks and defenses. By the time you get to epee you should have your footwork down, blade control down and your full arsenal of attacks and defenses at your disposal. Many fencers are gleefully happy to get rid of right of way. These are opinions and views that you will develop on your own as you grow with the sport.

One of the most basic attacks is the lunge. You start from the on-guard position, assuming you're right-handed. Shoot your front leg out, drop your body, and extend your arm as far forward as you can while bending in your knees. Keep your upper torso as straight as possible, and have your off hand fully extended as a counter balance.

When doing a lunge, you bring your body dangerously close to your opponent.

69. Illustration: Lunge with a tag

If your attack is ineffective, be prepared to block your opponent's blade and retreat. In your early days in the sport, you should practice frequent drills of advancing and retreating. Where you practice being in the on-guard position and then do a series of advances and retreats. And assuming you'll be doing most of your fencing on the fencing strip, the strip being very linear by its nature, you'll only be going in two directions, forward and backward; I do not recommend you entering a ring until you've had plenty of core practice on
the strip.

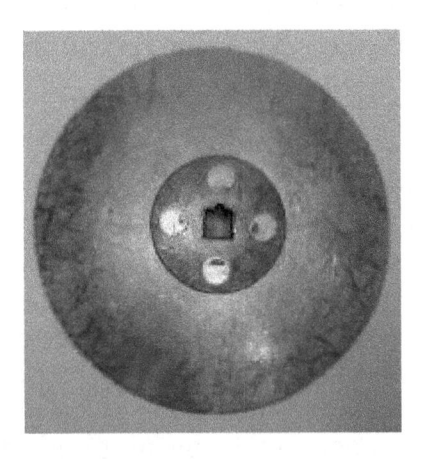

Figure 4: Foil Bell guard

A very basic defense is the parry. When your opponent thrusts his blade into your target area, you want to deflect it as quickly as possible, and do a counter attack quickly. If you want to effectively parry their blade, you want to deflect their blade, and then step into your opponent, and try to hit their target. Timing is everything in this sport. You will learn this as you advance in your skills and practice. Don't get discouraged if you get tagged often in most of your beginning bouts. You may begin to start feeling like a human pinnate. I was once there myself; you have to start somewhere. Familiarize yourself with your equipment, practice with it as much as you can. Take time selecting the proper weighted parts. Try the flexibility of many blades to find the one you like the most. You may spend a few dollars, and it may take you some time to experiment with stiffer or whippier blades. Heavier or lighter pommels and various types of assorted grips are all available; you'll have to decide which you like the most. Once you find the right combination of parts for you, stick with it. Don't lose faith.

Figure 5: Foil Bell guard pad

The benefits of this sport are that it is a wonderful full body cardiovascular workout. It's also a lot of fun. The biggest failure with most sports or exercises is they get repetitive and boring. No two fencers will be exactly alike, so you will constantly face a new opponent who will have new ways to attack and defend. And each person who fences is constantly changing and evolving. The beginning fencer employs very simply strategies as he's learning the game. And as he or she develops they make their strategies more complex and begin thinking on multiple levels. This is a good workout for the brain as well. In our modern age where computers do most of our work for us, and many of us have been reduced to automatons in the workplace, it forces your brain to think, and use its problem-solving skills. Think of it like chess on your feet.

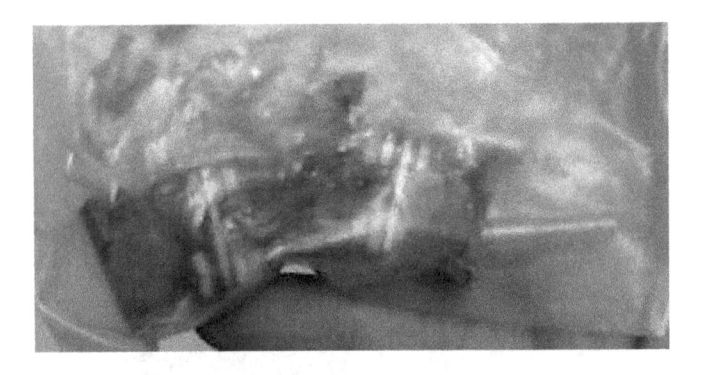

Figure 6: Component for Electric Fencing

If you plan on competing in tournaments, you'll need an electric weapon. When choosing this weapon, make sure its balanced out as closely as possible to your practice weapon.

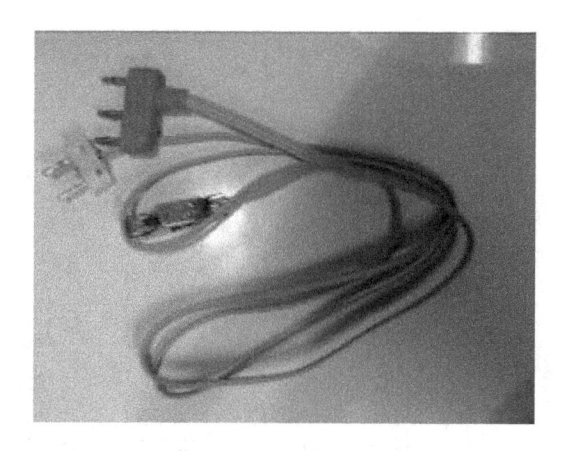

Figure 7: Body cords for Electronic weapon

If the weights do differ, it's better that your practice weapon be the heavier one, to give you an advantage in the long run. The reason being, when you step on the strip with your electric weapon your speed will increase. Everything you do will be just a bit quicker, and that could be what causes you to win. If it's the other way around, you'll be starting every electric scored match at a disadvantage. The balance to shoot for, however, is to have an electric foil and a practice foil that are virtually identical in every way: so that you will not have to adjust in any way from practice to tournament. The difference is the electric weapon has many small springs, wires and smaller parts that will get broken after so many tournaments. A practice blade has no moving parts whatsoever, and can be used again and again until the blade just snaps.

Figure 8: Electronic component that goes on uniform front

Practice blades often last a long time, and if used in tandem with the electric blade will prolong the life of your weapon.

Figure 9: Back of Electronic component for uniform

Watch the bend of your blade; this can be an indication that it is about to break. Your blade should be bent in a proper C curve (see photo). Oftentimes during heaving, booting your blade may develop a bend in the wrong direction, or an S type curve. This needs to be corrected immediately, because it will create weak points and places where the blade will be more likely to snap. After every tournament, make sure you're checking your blade for stress risers. These are chips or nicks in the length of your blade. Stress risers need to be sanded off or ground down, one of the two. Once a severe nick gets into the length of your blade, repeated nicks in the same area can result in your blade snapping in that spot. Just like in any sport, you want to maintain your equipment.

Figure 10: Unassembled epee blade

I have found four ways to do this. Take steel wool or a heavy grit sandpaper and go down the length of your blade. . Another method involves using a wet stone; run it across the blade until the nicks are worn off. In extreme circumstances with tremendous nicks, I've sometimes used a wet stone attachment on my dremel to grind down the nick. Truthfully, at times I'll use a combination of all four of these remedies. Over time you'll figure out what works best, and you'll be surprised at how it prolongs the life of your blade.

Don't forget to oil your blade after you've done this. Don't use anything heavier than 3 in one oil or WD-40. It will place a light coating on the blade. Before putting your blades away, take an oil rag and use it to periodically wipe the blades down. Ideally after each use, you should check for stress risers and deal with them appropriately. Oil the blades, wipe them down and put them away.

Figure 11: Unassembled foil blade

Care of your Equipment

You should ensure that your blades never get wet. Store them in a place where they will be able to stay cool and dry. Wetness on your blade will lead to rust on the metal. If it rusts too much, your blade will weaken. A bit of rust will show up from time to time, and you'll be able to get it off. You still need to check your blades and clean them from time to time by using steel wool, or even use metal sandpaper. If you are cleaning an electrical weapon you will need to be careful to not ruin the components.

Don't forget to also use a bit of oil, usually WD-40, or perhaps even three in one oil. This is going to help coat the blade to keep the rust away.

Figure 12: Inside of French grip steel

By placing your blade in a scabbard of some sort you'll be able to help protect it even further. Using a PVC pipe for this is easy to do, just go and buy it from your local hardware store and cut down to size.

Grips can wear out and need to be changed from time to time, no matter what sort of weapon you are using. In most cases this will only happen with a French grip or a sabre grip. Use of sports tape normally used for bats or tennis racquets will work just as well as more expensive tape you buy from a fencing company. Pistol grips don't normally need to be taped.

70. Illustration: Salute to judges and crowd second step

Of course, if you're always wearing your jacket to fence in it will need to be cleaned occasionally. One thing you need to make sure to do is after each use hang it up so that the sweat will dry out. This can keep you from having to wash it all the time. Plus, it will help keep mold from growing on your pants or jacket after you've sweat in them. You can use a mild disinfectant occasionally, to help keep the smell off the uniform; however, in the long run it most likely won't help out a ton.

Washing will be your best bet on making sure you don't smell out the competition while wearing your uniform. Don't use a lot of bleach on the clothes, even though you may want it looking bright white. Bleach will rot your material, and if you use too much of it

when washing your outfit, you're only going to end up
buying a new one sooner. With good maintenance,
your clothes could easily last you years.

Figure 13: Use with electronic components

For the mask, it's easily one of the most important
parts of equipment you should keep in good repair.
Always check to make sure there is no rust on the face
of your mask. Don't bundle up even a fencing glove
and let it sit inside of the mask. The sweat from the
glove, though it may not be much, could be just

enough to encourage the rust to start to grow. Check the bib to make sure there are no rips in it, if there are you can quickly repair it with a needle and thread.

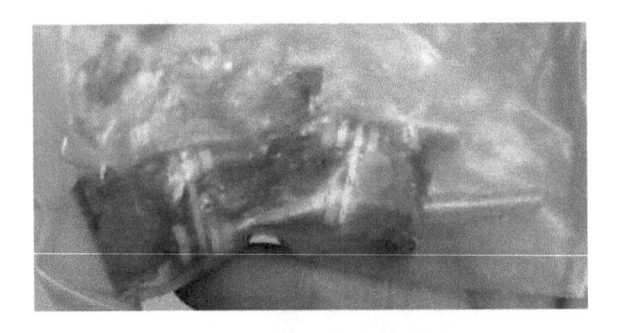

Figure 14: Electronic parts of weapon

Gloves are made from leather in many cases. Like the equipment listed above, they should be allowed to air out after you use them. Though it will not make them last forever, it could extend the life of a glove nicely.

Figure 15: Electronic weapon

Even though you may just be a beginner in fencing,

you could be considering a fencing bag. This is an item you should carefully consider, since they can be rather expensive. You have many choices out there, from a small standard bag that you carry, all the way up to a deluxe bag that can hold a bunch of equipment and you wheel around. Check out the bag as much as you can to ensure that you'll be happy with the layout of it. A lot of people don't like keeping their uniform with their swords; storing them separately will help keep punctures happening to your clothes, and is a good idea. However, not all bags are created equally; some will have a very bad layout, and will often have you placing all items in one slot. Again, with that you'll run a chance of a blade getting rust on an outfit, or something becoming dirty or even damaged. If you are serious about the sport and plan on attending tournaments where you want to look good, get a bag that has two separate compartments. But if you're just goofing around with friends, you can save money by getting a larger sized duffel bag or two and placing swords in one and clothing in the other.

Figure 16: Full electronic weapon

If you've placed things in your bag that are full of sweat take them out as soon as you can, so mold will not grow in your bag. Air out the clothes, but also air out the bag.

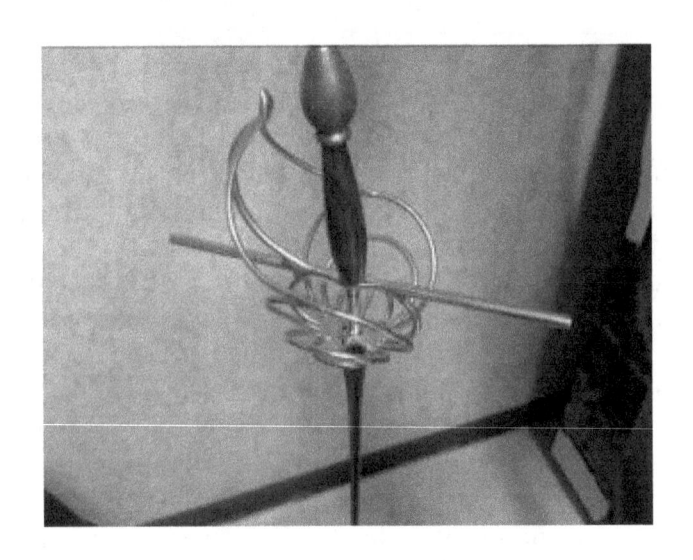

71. Illustration: Upper part of hilt, very protective of hand

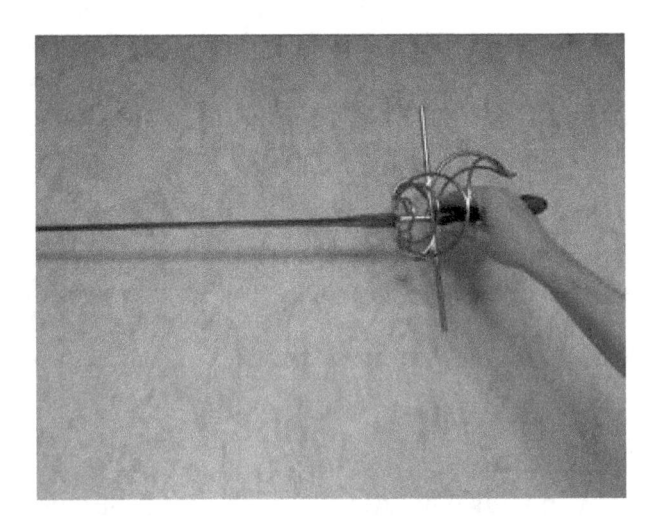

72. Illustration: Epee blade with fancy swept hilt

Other Books on Fencing: There are not many books out there about the subject of fencing; however, you can find a few. Besides this one, here are the others that I would suggest purchasing and reading.

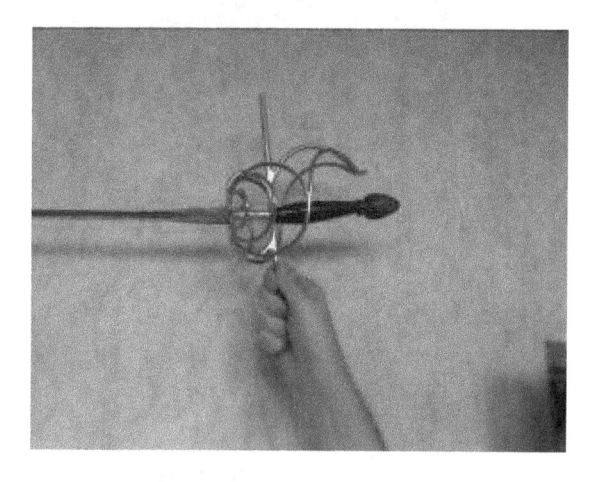

73. Illustration: Swept hilt, usable as French and Italian grip

"On Fencing" by Aldo Nadi, a great fencer of the past and a very helpful book that will teach you quite a bit, it's one of John's favorite books.

74. Illustration: On Fencing Aldo Nadi

For the foil specialist or even the beginner, another great choice would be "Foil Fencing" by Muriel Bower.

75. Illustration: Foil Fencing

Another great book that will just be interesting to read and give you a great history of swords and many of the welders of the past is "Sword" by Richard Cohen. In this book, you'll get a great history of Gladiators, Swashbucklers, Musketeers, Samurai, and Olympic champions of the past.

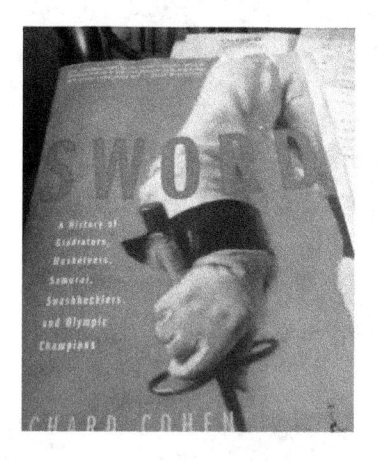

76. Illustration: Sword

Check out the steps to success you'll find in "Fencing" by Elaine Cheris.

77. Illustration: Fencing Steps to Success

Finally, your last choice for other books to help you learn more about the sport is "The art and science of fencing" by Nick Evangelista.

78. Illustration: The Art and Science of Fencing

Any of these books, used in conjunction with this one we've done should give you a great way to learn all you can about the sport. Becoming an expert won't mean just reading though; you will need to practice as much as you can.

Some places to look for equipment

There are many vendors who sell equipment for fencing online. Though you will have to find the one that works for you the best in the long run, here are some of them to check out. Depending on where you live you may be lucky enough to find a local store that may sell equipment; however, for most fencers who get into the sport, you will need to order from locations online.

Do be prepared to not only compare the quality of equipment, but the shipping cost as well. Some locations may end up charging you more to send their product then others, and this can make a big difference too.

Here are some of the ones we have ordered from before, but again this will be a decision that you will need to make on your own. In the long run, we have run into some that have sent us questionable products when it comes to quality. While still some places have seemed to add in additional shipping charges, these are places we will not use again, and have called them to question them about the things we've run into.

You can find great products from many places. Some will charge you for their name, and they are basically the same product you can find for cheaper at another location.

Look for great fencing gear at:

- Fence smart
- Absolute Fencing Equipment
- Triplett Fencing
- Blue Gauntlet
- Leon Paul
- Physical Chess

Again, those are only a few places where you will be able to find your gear. Compare prices, do a search on Google for Fencing equipment, and you'll find the locations all over the place.

Beware though not all fencing vendors are created equally though. Focus on the prices of the gear, quality, and shipping costs. In our minds, as long as we get products that are high quality and will last a long time we've done good. You will need to make sure to properly take care of any product that you buy. Check out the care instructions earlier in this book; it will help prolong the life of anything you buy online.

With proper care, your items will not have to be replaced very often. John has had a fencing mask he used for over fifteen years, finally after all that time we've bought a new mask. But it is still a product that he can use when we practice. The newer mask was purchased for events where he needs to have something that looks nicer.

Conclusion

John has been fencing for many years; he can assist you with all your needs. You can find more information via our Facebook page, Rogue Warrior Fencing. There is also a page on MySpace as well as a location that will be a site just for Rogue Warrior. Be sure to look us up and contact us if you have any specific questions to help you get started on a hobby that will help keep you fit and healthy. As well as something that could make you feel like a pirate of old ages.

This sport will offer you a lot, but you will need to be willing to learn. It will take time to advance your skills, but in the meantime while you are doing that you will also feel great.

79. Illustration: John Beeler

Get in shape with a sport that isn't the normal thing that you find out there. But something that will offer you an opportunity to not only use your body, but your mind in competing.

Christy, though a beginning fencer, has learned a lot from the teaching of John. Together they plan on making a business that will offer to the everyday person a chance to experience this sport. With very little investment on your part you can find a new and great way to get into shape.

80 Illustration: John and Christy getting ready to fence

So, try a new sport, one that used to be for the rich only, but can now be enjoyed just as much by all people around the globe. With patience and time, you can become a great fencer, one who could collect trophies and praise from your community. If you are a younger person with training and time you may one day even be able to compete in the Olympics.

Be sure to not only check out the various spots online where you will be able to learn more about this sport, but the books we've mentioned as well.

When you do decide to get into this sport, be sure to go to a qualified instructor. In some locations, they may be a bit harder to find. In that case you should be able to take this manual and the other books that are out there and give yourself a great way to begin this sport. In time, you may one day decide that you will want to become a coach of this sport as well.

About the Expert

John Beeler has been fencing for over 21 years, and is an avid lover of the sport. He has been teaching Christine the sport for almost a year now. With each of their loves of the sport, they thought it would be nice to let others know how easy it was to get into fencing. Between John's knowledge of the sport and Christine's writing ability, they have put together an instruction manual that can have anyone, of any age beginning the new hobby of fencing. John and Christine are also hoping to one day begin their own fencing school.

HowExpert publishes quick 'how to' guides on all topics from A to Z by everyday experts. Visit HowExpert.com to learn more.

Recommended Resources

- HowExpert.com – Quick 'How To' Guides on All Topics from A to Z by Everyday Experts.
- HowExpert.com/free – Free HowExpert Email Newsletter.
- HowExpert.com/books – HowExpert Books
- HowExpert.com/courses – HowExpert Courses
- HowExpert.com/clothing – HowExpert Clothing
- HowExpert.com/membership – HowExpert Membership Site
- HowExpert.com/affiliates – HowExpert Affiliate Program
- HowExpert.com/writers – Write About Your #1 Passion/Knowledge/Expertise & Become a HowExpert Author.
- HowExpert.com/resources – Additional HowExpert Recommended Resources
- YouTube.com/HowExpert – Subscribe to HowExpert YouTube.
- Instagram.com/HowExpert – Follow HowExpert on Instagram.
- Facebook.com/HowExpert – Follow HowExpert on Facebook.